Spirituality & Sexuality

A Godly Perspective

Kelvin K. Lucas

HIS GLORY CREATIONS PUBLISHING, LLC
WENDELL

His Glory Creations Publishing, LLC
Wendell, North Carolina

Copyright © 2018 by Kelvin K. Lucas

ALL RIGHTS RESERVED
No portion of this publication may be reproduced, stored in any electronic system, or transmitted in any form or by any means, electronic, mechanical, photocopy, recording, or otherwise, without written permission from the publisher. Brief quotations may be used in literary reviews. Unauthorized reproduction of any part of this work is illegal and is punishable by law.

All Scripture quotations are taken from The Holy Bible, King James Version (KJV). Cambridge Edition: 1769; King James Bible Online, 2018. www.kingjamesbibleonline.org. All rights reserved worldwide.

ISBN: 978-1-7327227-1-2
Library of Congress Number: 2018910721

Printed in the United States of America
10 9 8 7 6 5 4 3 2 1

DEDICATION

To those who seek to live life the way God intended it through Jesus Christ.

Real...Practical...Simply Victorious!

"Now therefore ye are no more strangers and foreigners, but fellow-citizens with the ...household of God...built upon the foundation of...Jesus Christ himself being the chief cornerstone..."

Ephesians 2:19-20

CONTENTS

	Acknowledgments	7
1	Relationship 101	9
2	It's a Spiritual Thing	27
3	Sexuality an Honest Conversation	39
4	The Joseph Connection	51
5	There is a Potiphar's Wife	55
6	The Takedown & Recovery	61
7	Lay the Chief Cornerstone	67
	About the Author	75

Spirituality & Sexuality

A Godly Perspective

As you read the book, I will share with you some of my personal experiences in life during a segment entitled, **"Tee Time"**.

I welcome you to reflect upon your own life experiences in the **"Measure It Up"** segments. These are designed to help you engage in thought provoking moments that may allow the Lord to minister to certain areas in your life.

ACKNOWLEDGMENTS

I want to thank my wife Felicia, our kids and my mother for their unwavering support. Also, to those who have supported our ministry efforts over the years and believed in our cause to serve the needs of others…this one is for you!

Spirituality & Sexuality

A Godly Perspective

1- Relationship 101

The two most important aspects of who you are as a human being can be categorized into two components: SPIRITUALITY & SEXUALITY. You are both a spiritual and sexual being, and the challenge is how do you successfully manage both components as they co-exist within you. Society has attempted to define these two components based upon doing whatever makes you happy. But at the end of the day, will the pursuit of that happiness measure up to the standard by which you were created? You must seek to understand what that standard is and by whom has the standard been established. True Spirituality and Sexuality comes from God. He is the originator of all creation, and he has created the standard by which you must frame your life under his divine authority.

Let's take this journey together as you seek to understand these two aspects of human life and rise to the challenge of incorporating them into a working model you can apply to many different areas in your life.

Spirituality and Sexuality deal with the idea of what is called RELATIONSHIP. Relationship is how you interact with or relate to other individuals. There are different types of relationships within our society:

*Husband/Wife

* Parent/Child

*Employer/Employee

*Siblings

*Boyfriend/Girlfriend

In general, a relationship is like a clock that hangs on the wall. Just as the hands at the center of the clock move forward with time, so must you serve as the hands at the center of your relationships to help them move forward. There is nothing worse in life than a sour relationship going nowhere fast. Time waits for no one, and it is vital to understand that as time moves forward in progression, so must your relationships progress as well. There are 5 key components to consider when moving a relationship forward. These components coincide with the following times on the clock:

12 o'clock=**Time**, 3 o'clock= **Choice**, 5 o'clock=**Effort**, 7 o'clock=**Emotions** and 9 o'clock=**Physical Reality**.

Society often teaches that the most important assets in life are: money, real estate, clothing, and automobiles. However, I want to challenge your thinking and suggest to you that the two most important assets you will ever have in life are *TIME*

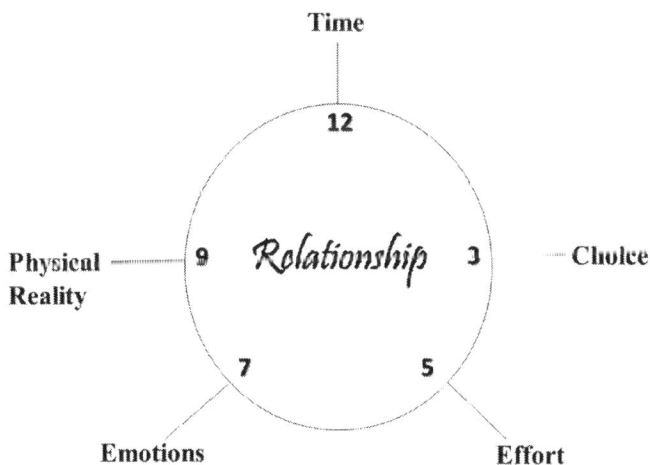

and the power of *CHOICE*. **TIME** is important because it gives you the opportunity to live and learn. Each day that you wake up represents the time that has been given to you. Somewhere around the world today, someone didn't wake up. Unfortunately, they passed away. Their time to live has expired. But, if you are able to read this book, then you should CELEBRATE because you are alive and have been given more time to experience what God has to offer you! Now the questions become WHO, WHAT, WHEN, and WHERE.

Who do I share time with?
_____

What do I do with the time I have?
_____

When do I need to do it?
_____

Where (what area(s) in my life or physical location) should I devote time towards?_____

Successful relationships hinge upon the answers to those questions. Now regardless of what type of relationship it is, those thought-provoking questions demand the use of your second important asset of *CHOICE*.

CHOICE is simply how you use your time to impact your life and the lives of others. It is the direction in which you lead yourself and depending on the type of relationships you are in the direction in which you can inspire others to follow. Husbands have the responsibility of making wise choices when leading their marriages, parents have the same responsibility when leading their children, employers must use profitable decision making when leading their employees, older siblings have the responsibility of being positive role models and leading their younger siblings and if you're considering dating, then both individuals involved owe it to each other to bring value added choices to the table.

Value is added to a relationship when those involved make choices that reflect God's standard of serving and take into consideration the wellbeing of others. In other words, you can't be selfish and expect your relationships to progress. You must be willing to sacrifice yourself at various times and commit to helping improve the quality of life for someone else.

When I think of value-added relationships, I think of the Biblical examples of Noah (**Genesis 6**) and Moses (**Genesis 25-27**). Each of these men embraced the purpose of God for their life to serve and had the wellbeing of others in mind while working that purpose out! Noah chose to follow God's blueprint to build the ark which served as a place of safety during the flood for him and his family and those who chose to enter it. Moses chose to follow God's blueprint to build The Tabernacle, which served as a mobile place of worship for him, his family and the children of Israel as they made their exodus from Egypt into the wilderness. These men added value to the lives of others because they helped produce something that improved and preserved the quality of life. Your life is a gift from God. Maximize it by serving him and helping others.

****Tee ↑Time! –*The choices that you make in life should ultimately lead to producing something that improves the quality of life for others. For example, when I volunteered to serve as the PTA President at my children's middle school, I maximized the community relationship by collaborating with the Guidance department to introduce a Leadership and Creative Writing Initiative. During that two-year period, both initiatives were very successful and over 35 students benefited by learning the basic principles of leadership and some became published authors through the assistance of my wife and author Felicia Lucas.*

******Measure** 🖊 **it Up!** – Can you recall an experience where you were able to add value to a relationship? What was the outcome?

_____

_____

_____

_____

_____

_____

_____

_____

_____

_____

_____

_____

_____

_____

_____

The most active part of any relationship occurs at 5 o'clock.

EFFORT is an action word. In life, you can make choices all day long, but if you do not put any effort behind them, your choices mean nothing and your relationships along with the hands on your clock will come to a complete halt.

Good effort in relationships require time and comes in forms such as:

Effective Listening & Observation*- Putting forth the effort to listen and observe in a relationship allows you to understand what the needs are. Sometimes your best effort in a relationship can be non-physical and non-verbal, where you don't do or say anything. You simply listen and watch.*

Being a husband and father continues to teach me to listen more and talk less. If I am doing all the talking, then when do my wife and kids have a chance to participate in the conversation? Do you dominate the conversations within your relationships or do you allow opportunity for others to share how they feel?

I recall my wife said to me in a conversation one day, "We have been married for years and have nothing to show for it." In my mind, I thought that a house, food, clothing, and vehicles were enough, but God challenged my listening and thinking. God helped me to understand that she desired our marriage relationship to expand beyond where it was and become more enjoyable.

Once I took the **TIME** to understand what she meant, I **CHOSE** to put more **EFFORT** into planning more date nights and other fun excursions that added value to our marriage.

I also leveraged that mentality with my kids and became more actively involved in volunteering at their school, serving as a coach for their little league teams, and planning more fun activities.

I struggled early in my parenting relationship, because I would use my work schedule as an excuse. But once again

God challenged me to look to him for strength and put forth the effort to become more involved. I am glad I did because it has given our family some great memories as well as networking opportunities to cultivate what we do through our community outreach ministry, Take It By Force Ministries, Inc. (TIBF).

Goal Planning and Follow Through - *After you understand what the needs are in the relationship, put forth effort by setting goals that meet those needs. You must stay focused on your goals and not allow obstacles to hinder your progress. Time is never hindered by obstacles, it just calculates them into the process. You must do the same thing! Go after your goals and advance that relationship to 7 o'clock!*

I recall when I would plan activities for my wife and kids, unexpected obstacles would always arise and cast a shadow of doubt. Sometimes the weight of those obstacles would seem to outweigh the excitement for the plans. But I remained positive, asked the Lord for strength and made the plans happen!

Setting positive goals and following through with them gives you a sense of accomplishment while at the same time making your relationships more enjoyable.

If you take care of business at 12, 3 and 5 o'clock respectively, then you are right on time at 7 o'clock! The **EMOTIONAL** component can be a good indicator of what happens at those previous times. If the TIME was taken to make wise CHOICES and EFFORT was put forth to make those choices a reality, then the emotional results at 7 o'clock could possibly be happiness, joy, peace, high self-esteem, and a positive attitude. However, depending on what life throws your way, you can also experience stress, anxiety, fear, and frustration.

******Tee** |**Time!** *–Being married for over 21 years challenges me to incorporate time, choice, and effort into my daily routine. Sometimes it's difficult to manage being a husband, father, and pastor because those three titles* *require different levels of responsibility from just one person. I think that is where I as a human being with multiple levels of functioning, coincide with the image and likeness of God, who exists as the Father, Son, & Holy Spirit. He is one God with three unique levels of functioning. He recognized the need of humanity to be rescued from the power of sin and gave of himself in the form of his son Jesus Christ, to meet the need. Therefore, he is a credible resource when it comes to meeting the need during those critical moments in relationships.*

I recall a time when my wife and I had a huge argument before she went out of town on a business trip. I was emotionally frustrated but recognized the need for healing the situation. So, on the day of her return, while working in the office, the Lord instructed me to cancel my plans for the evening, ask my mom to watch the kids and meet my wife for a romantic evening away from the house. I did what he said, and the evening was wonderful. The situation was a bump in the road, but the Lord helped me to smooth it out and manage the: **who** (my wife), **what** (meet her), **when** (upon her return) & **where** (nice hotel).

No relationship is perfect. But the goal is to reach some ***PHYSICAL REALITY*** that can be measured at 9 o'clock. Typically, there are two realities at 9 o'clock: success and failure. If the reality is successful...be thankful. If it is failure, learn from it and move towards 12 o'clock (A New Day!) keeping in mind, the lessons learned that contributed to the success or failure.

******Measure** ✏ **it Up!** - Are there areas in your life that hinder you from adding value to your relationships? Have you chosen to put forth the effort to address those challenging areas? If so what was the outcome? If not, what are you waiting for?

_____

_____

_____

_____

***Tee Time!** - *My biggest challenge growing up as the only child, was to resist the tendency to be selfish. I struggled with selfishness early in my marriage. But the more knowledgeable I became of God's word, the better I became at understanding my role as a husband was to help give form, identity, and life to the embryo of ideas, goals, and passions that are within my wife.*

Relationships are essential ingredients in life. They give your life purpose and function. Ask God to teach you how to manage your relationships successfully and remember that a life well lived is one that adds value and inspires others to achieve greatness!

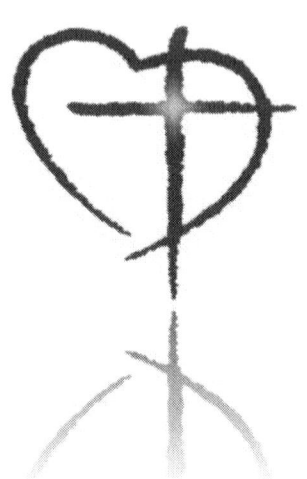

2- It's a Spiritual Thing

The neat thing about the relationship clock model is that it can be applied to different aspects of your life, to help provide a practical blueprint for living. In this chapter, we will apply the model to SPIRITUALITY.

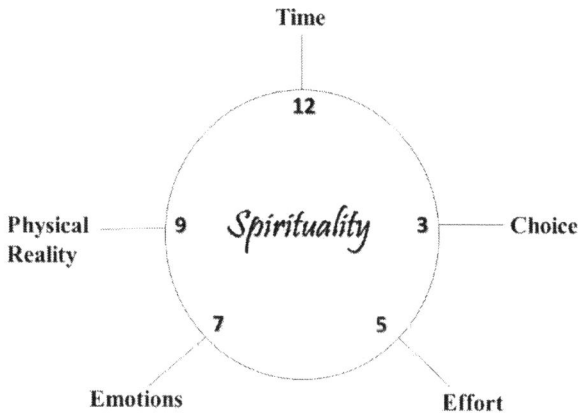

Spirituality deals with how you manage your relationship with God. To understand this relationship, it's important to understand the prefix of the word spirituality, which is **Spirit**. A spirit is an actual being that dwells within an individual and has a direct impact on that person's life. The Bible says in **John 4:24**, *"God is a Spirit...."* The influence that the Spirit of God has on an individual can be read in **Genesis 2:7** where we learn that God formed man from the dust of the ground and breathed into his nostrils the breath of life. All life comes from God, and he has the capacity to dwell within you as well as the ability to have a positive influence on your life. Let's take a moment and...

******Measure** ✏ **it Up!** - Did you know that you have a measure of God's grace within you? It's called the breath of life. It belongs to him, but he is allowing you TIME to use it for a while. What an opportunity! Make the most of it.

Spirituality is such an important part of your life because it can give you guidance concerning the choices you make in life. However, you must be willing to seek out that guidance through your relationship with God. In the Bible, **Proverbs 2:3** teaches that you must cry out and seek knowledge and understanding which comes from God (**v.6**). Obtaining knowledge and understanding from God is essential to having successful relationships as well as a successful life in general.

The journey towards managing a successful relationship with God begins with taking the **TIME** to **CHOOSE** his son Jesus Christ as your Lord and personal Savoir. This is so important and if you have been wanting to give your life to the Lord but didn't know how just say the following prayer:

"Dear Lord Jesus, I believe that you died on the cross for my sins and that you were raised on the third day. I repent of my sins, I lift my hands and I receive you into my heart and mind right now as my Lord and personal Savoir. In Jesus name, Amen!"

If you prayed that prayer and meant it from your heart, then go ahead and give God a **PRAISE!!!** You just received Jesus Christ and are well on your way to managing a successful relationship with God. The next step is to find a good Bible teaching church and begin to attend on a regular basis, so you can fellowship with others and develop your spirituality.

******Tee** ↑**Time!** - *I remember when I gave my life to the Lord Jesus at age 13. It was the best decision I ever made. From my teenage years to my years as being a husband, father, and pastor, my relationship with Christ has been the foundation for my success.*

Now becoming spiritually mature means, you must choose to devote the necessary time it takes to grow that relationship. This means taking the opportunity to study your Bible, attend church consistently and spend time praying for knowledge and understanding as you model your life after Christ. Modeling after Christ requires **EFFORT**! It also requires you to put forth emotional and physical energy.

EMOTIONAL energy comes into play when you must deal with the different feelings you sometimes have in life. Feelings such as fear, doubt, anger, and frustration can play a part in your life, but if you don't manage them correctly, they can lead to negative results. Do not allow yourself to take on the identities of the negative emotions but overcome them by renewing your mind.

Renewal of the mind comes by modeling the mindset of Christ. The Apostle Paul writes in **Philippians 2:5-7**, *"Let this mind be in you which was also in Christ Jesus who...made himself of no reputation and took...the form of a servant..."*

Christ was not concerned with making a name for himself but focused on serving the needs of others. When you serve, it can shift the focus from your negative emotions and challenge you to **add value** to someone's life.

As you are making that **PHYSICAL** investment into someone's life, you are mentally:

- Overcoming *fear* with **Faith** which is the main ingredient in your relationship with God, The Bible says in **Hebrews 11:6**, *"But without faith it is* *impossible to please him..*" Faith says, "**I can add value to someone!**"

- Overcoming *doubt* with **Hope** which is an expectation of greater things. Hope encourages you to say, **"I will add value to someone!"**

- Overcoming *anger* with **Peace** of mind knowing that, **"I did add value to someone!"**

- Overcoming *frustration* with **Patience** which is the experience you gain from the process and the motivation behind your next assignment. It says, **"Let's do it again!"**

I have applied this model to various areas in my own life. From managing the family budget, planning a weekend or anniversary getaway, to planning a PTA function, I thank God for the testimony…. I can do it……I will do it…I did do it…. Let's do it again!

******Tee** ⛳ **Time!** - *Whenever I volunteer within the community, it helps me overcome my worries, because my mind is focused on what can I do to help encourage faith, hope, peace, and patience. Whether I'm visiting a school campus or a retirement center, I realize the more I serve the needs of others, the more God enables me to manage and overcome my own obstacles.*

Serving others not only helps me emotionally but it gives me a chance to physically put into motion what I learn and teach about on Sundays! I think it's about that time! Let's....

******Measure** ✏ **it Up!** - Are you involved in any volunteer program on a regular basis? If not, what are some areas in your community that you feel strongly about improving?

_____

_____

_____

_____

Contact a business or organization that specializes in that cause and ask if they need volunteer assistance. You could make a world of difference.... Christ did!

Take it from me, if God can help me overcome my introvert personality and utilize me to serve in ways that I never thought of, especially as a PTA President, then he can use you too!

A great way to conclude this chapter is to look at a very familiar scripture and apply it to the clock model introduced at the beginning of the chapter.

John 3:16 says, *"For God so loved the world, that he gave his only begotten son, that whosoever believeth in him should not perish, but have everlasting life."*

Utilizing the following list of words from John 3:16, fill in the parenthesis on the clock.

- God=12, Loved=7, Gave=5, Believe=3, Life=9

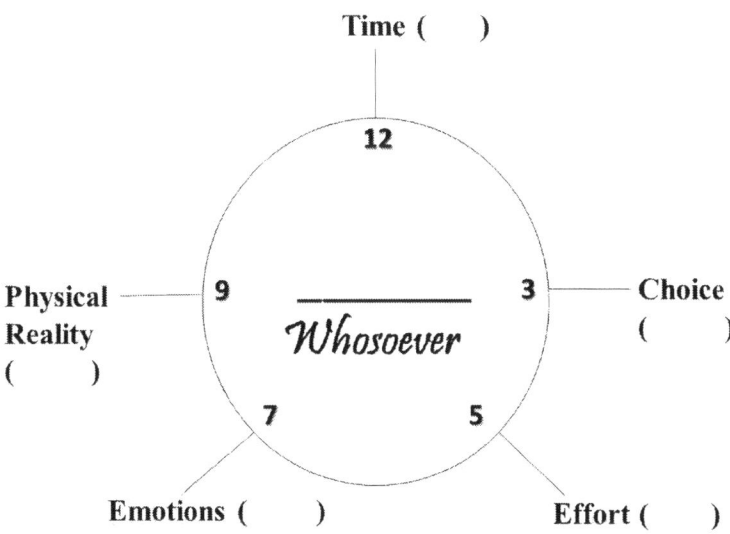

Now write your name on the whosoever line and look at the model for a moment.

The diagram indicates that **God** is ***time***, and he showed you the ***emotion*** of **love** by putting forth ***effort*** to **give** of himself in the form of Jesus Christ. When you ***choose*** to accept and believe in Christ, you are laying the chief cornerstone foundation that is essential for your reality called *life*! As you reflect upon the five areas on the clock mentioned in this chapter, understand that God has already implemented them by giving you the very best he had. He gave himself. He wants you to do the same.

Choose to implement this model and make the most of the time God provides, by putting forth effort to develop your spirituality and let him use you. If you are ready, then lift your hands, open your mouth and shout, "Use me LORD!"

Spirituality & Sexuality

A Godly Perspective

3- Sexuality an Honest Conversation

One of the most sensitive subjects known to humanity is sexuality. Without sex, the human race would be nonexistent. Sexuality deals with how you manage your attraction to the opposite sex. It is important to realize that sex was ordained by God for a purpose. That purpose is a meaningful RELATIONSHIP between a husband and his wife (**Genesis 4:1-2**) with the capacity to form the institution known as the family.

Before Adam became a sexual being, he was a spiritual being first, because God transferred his spirit into the form of man and because of the transfer, Adam became a living spiritual being. This is a classic example of what true relationship does. It gives form, identity and life! That's adding value.

******Measure** ✏ **it Up!** - When you are in a relationship, what can you bring to the table other than the physical act of sex, that will add value to the process?

_____

_____

_____

_____

After God created Eve, Adam married her, and they engaged in the Godly ordained physical act of sex between a husband and his wife. Adam and Eve represent God's intended purpose for the institution of marriage and sex. Anything beyond that purpose does not meet God's standard **(Leviticus 18:22)**, **(1Corinthians 6:18-20, 7:2)**. Spirituality must be the governing source which teaches you what sexuality is all about. You can't look to the government, educational system, friends, social media or pornography to fulfill this purpose.

The key to meaningful sexuality is a STRONG spiritual

relationship with God through Christ. As you **continuously** develop your spirituality, you are creating an asset that will help you manage not just your sexuality, but other areas in your life such as finances and career objectives. Now sexuality is more than just the physical act of sex itself. As the diagram below shows, the physical component is only one of five. First of all, managing your attraction to the opposite sex takes **TIME**.

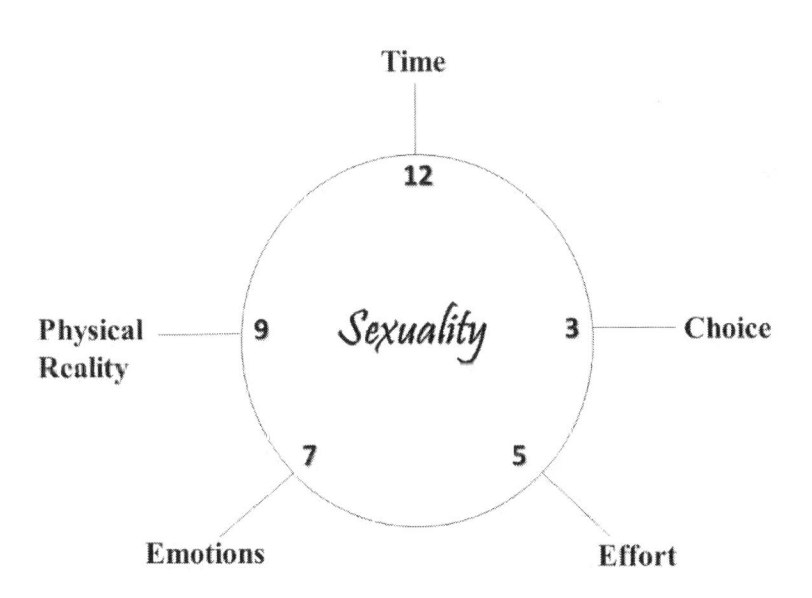

```
                    Time
                     |
                     12
                  
  Physical  ——— 9   Sexuality   3 ——— Choice
  Reality
                  7           5
                  |           |
               Emotions     Effort
```

Get to know the individual's:

- Parents
- Do they have a **relationship** with the Lord?
- Hobbies (Do you have anything in common other than a physical attraction?)
- Does the person have a positive attitude or are they a trouble maker?
- Any long and short-term goals
- Do they have a JOB or career aspirations?

The above-mentioned areas help shape an individual's personality, which can go far beyond the physical appearance.

You may find yourself attracted to more than one person. If that is the case, then the smart thing to do is to **CHOOSE** ONE person that best suits your interests and get to know the individual. This part of sexuality can be classified as dating. Now please make sure that the person is not already married or dating someone else. If so, leave the person alone and move on! But getting back to my point... getting to know a person is more than just a physical attraction. It should also include a personality attraction, which occurs when you are drawn to the person's inner qualities. It's about that time...

******Tee** **Time!** - *I remember when I first saw my wife, Felicia....I was a senior in college preparing to fly to Atlanta for a job interview. Before leaving my dorm, I prayed and asked the Lord to show me my wife on this trip...Soon after I arrived at the airport, I saw this young lady coming down the concourse, but I didn't think anything of her. However, when I boarded the plane I noticed someone across the aisle was looking over my shoulder at my travel itinerary....it was the same young lady I had seen earlier. Immediately I thought to myself, "This is a nosy girl!" After we landed, I learned that she was interviewing with the same company. We both were hired and ended up training together in Charlotte, NC. During that time, we really got to know each other, and I was really drawn to her personality. Physically* *she was attractive, but I was really drawn to her inner qualities: she had a sense of humor, she was funny, she didn't curse, and she loved the Lord. The rest is* **HIStory....HERstory....OURstory!**

Now spirituality can play a key role when it comes to dating. Check out **Proverbs 2:11-19** which teaches that Godly wisdom and understanding (strong spirituality) can help you avoid engaging in a dating relationship with someone who may have a negative impact on your life. Notice I said, "Can help" because you must make the final choice to be in the relationship. Sisters be careful of men who may look and talk fine as wine, but ain't worth a dime! Brothers just because it looks tight don't make it right! What looks good to you may not be good for you! Don't get so hooked on the outward appearance and overlook the inward characteristics.

******Tee ⏐Time!** *- I recall entering a relationship with a young lady when I was in my teens (long before I met my* *wife). It was a disastrous relationship because I was attracted to the physical aspect of who she was...not her personality. The relationship hindered me spiritually, and I found myself living outside of God's purpose for my life. I understood Godly wisdom and understanding, however, I wanted to do my own thing, which led down the wrong path. I didn't do a great job of managing that relationship, because I allowed my sexuality (choice in dating partner) to negatively impact my spirituality.*

Your turn...

******Measure ✎ it Up!** - What was your worst dating experience? Why did you choose to date the person? Did you continue to use the same standard for other dating choices or did your standards change?

_____   _____

_____

_____

Successful dating takes **EFFORT**. This means getting to know your dating partner and being a positive influence. A good way to get to know your dating partner is by planning some type of planned activity (movies, dining, bowling, miniature golf, go-carts or church).

******Tee Time!** - *I remember the first movie my wife and I went to see when we were training together in Charlotte. When we got to the theatre she sat two seats over from me. A few weeks later we went to the movies again....this time she sat right next to me...I thought to myself, "What is this girl doing?....Am I having that much of a positive influence on her".....halfway through the movie she put her head on my shoulder...I thought to myself, "Oh ok....well maybe I am having a positive influence on her!" She and I laugh about it all the time. We were having fun getting to know each other!*

A successful dating relationship requires a lot of **EMOTIONAL** energy. This type of energy comes into play when you must deal with the different desires you feel towards the opposite sex when dating. A common desire you may feel when dating is FORNICATION. Fornication is sexually based activity between two unmarried individuals. If not managed correctly, the **REALITY** this type of behavior can lead to serious consequences such as pregnancy and sexually transmitted diseases (STDs).

An effective way to manage fornication is to pray and discuss it with your dating partner. Use the Bible (**1Corinthians 6:18-20**) as a reference to understand God's perspective on abstaining from such behavior. If there is no mutual agreement to abstain from such behavior, then it is best to end the dating relationship.

Strong spirituality provides a foundation that can help yield good decision making towards sexuality decisions (i.e., respectable dating partner, abstinence). However, the individual still must choose what to do. If the decision is made to go down the wrong road, you must be willing to get yourself together and change the course of direction.

As a spiritual and sexual being, the challenge in life is to manage each component as they co-exist within you. I want to share with you a few characters in the Bible and see how spirituality and sexuality co-existed in their life situation. The goal is to see how the individual managed each component and try to make a personal connection that may help you.

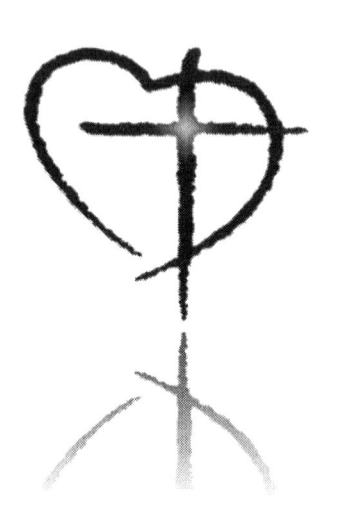

4- The Joseph Connection

Take a look at a situation in **Genesis 39** concerning a man whose name was Joseph. Joseph was a son of Israel and loved very much by his father. However, his brothers didn't like him. They were mean to him and threw him in a pit. While there, a group of men lifted Joseph out of the pit and sold him to a man named Potiphar.

Now the Bible says in **Genesis 39:2**, *"....and the Lord was with Joseph."* The word WITH is important because it implies some level of RELATIONSHIP. When you are in a relationship, you are with that person on a consistent basis. You hang out and talk with the person. They know you, and you know them. There is a connection there. For Joseph, this was his **SPIRITUALITY** component, because it implies that the Lord was with him. Being with the Lord is much like a husband being with his wife. Just as the husband has the capacity to impregnate his wife with a seed that produces a child, so does the Lord impregnate those who are in relationship with him. He fills them with the seeds of wisdom and understanding through the Holy Spirit which can be used to manage everyday life.

Now look at the next part of the verse which reads... *"and he (Joseph) was a prosperous man."* What you see here in Joseph is a man who had a spiritual connection with God, and was very successful, despite the fact that his brothers didn't like him.

Key #1- A strong spiritual relationship with God through his son Jesus Christ will help you succeed when others want you to fail. You must be willing to allow God to fill you with his wisdom and understanding. **Genesis 39:2** reads, *"And his master saw that the Lord was with him and that the Lord made all he did to prosper in his hand."* Joseph's boss, Potiphar noticed Joseph's spirituality and the success that came with it.

***Key #2*-** When you are full of God's wisdom and understanding you bring a certain level of quality to the table. In a relationship, that is called, "Value Added." Strive to live a life that is humble and pleasing to God, and he will enable you to achieve great things in life and add value to your environment. **Genesis 39:4** says, *"And Joseph found grace in his (Potiphar) sight, and he (Potiphar) made him overseer over his house and all that he had, he put into his hand."* God had given Joseph favor in Potiphar's eyes. Potiphar had entrusted Joseph to manage the affairs of his house because he knew the positive results Joseph could produce.

***Key #3*-** As you learn how to manage your spirituality successfully, God's favor will provide doors of opportunity. In the first part of this chapter, we saw how Joseph's spirituality played a key role in his success at Potiphar's house. Not bad for a brother who was thrown into a pit and later sold off!

Spirituality & Sexuality

A Godly Perspective

5- There is a Potiphar's Wife

No matter how strong you may be spiritually. You are still a human being, and you will be tested. One such test will come through your sexuality. In life, you will be confronted with your own sexual emotions as well as the sexual emotions of others that will be very tempting. These human emotions seek to please the sexual nature of the individual.

The challenge is how to manage those emotions. Now Joseph was doing well at Potiphar's house, and others took notice, especially Potiphar's wife.

In **Genesis 39:7** it says, *"and it came to pass after these things that Potiphar's wife cast her eyes upon Joseph and said lie with me."* Here we have an example where Joseph was confronted with the opportunity to have sex with a married woman. That form of relationship is called adultery. Adultery is a sexual relationship between two individuals, where at least one of the persons is married.

******Measure** ✏ **it Up!** - Have you ever been invited to engage in a sexual act that you knew was wrong? How did you respond?

_____

_____

_____

_____

_____

_____

Joseph must rely upon his spirituality to navigate him through this test. Godly wisdom enables him to recognize that her invitation is evil and to engage in such activity would be a sin against God. Potiphar's house for Joseph represents two dynamics coexisting in the same house: spiritual success and sexual testing.

Key Point-Your physical being is a type of Potiphar's house, where your spirituality represents the opportunity for great success, and your sexuality represents the opportunity for great testing.

Two dynamics coexist within the same house (your physical being). Just as Potiphar's wife constantly challenged Joseph (**v.10**) and grabbed him (**v.12**), so will your sexuality challenge you with a **Potiphar's wife** in the form of ungodly thoughts, individuals, music, movies, books, magazines and social media. You must realize that Potiphar's wife comes to grab your spirituality and take it down.

Joseph realized that her proposal was wicked and sinful (**v.9**) and responded by getting up and leaving the scene (**v.12**). You too must learn to think likewise when confronted with sexual temptations and other temptations in general. Get up (**mentally** and **physically**) and move yourself to a higher level of functioning! Pray, take a cold shower, cook, clean, exercise, do the laundry, mow the lawn, water the flowers, or read a good book. Do something positive to focus your attention elsewhere.

The Bible encourages us in **James 4:7** which says, *"Submit yourselves to God. Resist the devil (temptation), and he will flee from you."* Now also understand, you don't have to wait for the devil to flee from you, you can flee from him.

In Joseph's case submitting to God prompted Joseph himself to make a move. He didn't wait for Mrs. Potiphar (temptation) to leave, Joseph took it upon himself to get out first!

Now the devil (temptation) will be back. That's his job (**1Peter 5:8**). But your job is to be spiritually sober enough to choose the right course of action. It took effort on Joseph's part not to go along for the ride with Mrs. Potiphar. He saw his relationship with God as being more important than a cheap thrill! You must do the same.

But what if you don't want to focus your attention on that which is good and choose to go along for the ride? Well, let's take a look at one such example in a man named David.

6- The Takedown & Recovery

King David was a man who understood the importance of spirituality. But he also knew what it felt like to be confronted with sexual temptations as well. One evening in **2Samuel 11:2** he went to the rooftop of his house and saw an attractive woman bathing. He learned that the woman Bathsheba was the wife of his soldier Uriah. David was confronted with the desire to have sexual relations with a married woman. How did he respond? He decided to go along for the ride.

He sent a message to Bathsheba inviting her to come over. She accepted the invite, and as a result, they had sex, and she became pregnant (**vv. 3-5**)

What this example shows is how a sexually related thought can originate within the mind of a spiritually minded individual and **take down** the spirituality component of the individual just long enough to achieve its objective. Be mindful of individuals, thoughts, and patterns that want to take down your spirituality just long enough to accomplish their agenda because after the agenda is over you still have to deal with the consequences! Unlike Joseph, David chose a different approach when confronted with the sexuality test. Now he was in a mess!

David tried to fix the mess himself, but his failed attempts resulted in the murder of Bathsheba's husband (**vv. 6-15**) and the death of the child she had borne to David (**2Samuel 12: 15-19**). When your spirituality is taken down by the desires of your flesh, it opens the door for death to come in.

But when David found himself at his lowest point, he turned to his spirituality (which was taken down initially), to raise him back up. In **2Samuel 12:20** it says that David arose from the earth, changed his clothes and went into the house of the Lord to worship. The worship experience is not described in 2Samuel 12, but **Psalm 51** provides some insight on how David was feeling during this season in his life, and what a worship conversation with the Lord would sound like.

Your relationship with the Lord teaches you to have a repentant heart when you fall. In **Psalm 51: 1-2**, David asked the Lord to have mercy upon him and shows a desire to be clean. That's the *first* step to recovery. You must have a desire to be clean.

Secondly, in verses (**3-5**) David admitted that in his sinful nature he made an error in his thinking which led to his sin against God. Acknowledging your sin and the negative results it can have on your spiritually, along with the desire to be clean, beckons you to cry out to the Lord even more just as David did in verses (**7-8**).

The beauty of this worship experience is in verses (**10-13**). David did not want God to throw him away, but he wanted the Lord to keep working on him, so that when he recovered, he could help someone else (**v.13**).

David's example is a practical model of how your spirituality (relationship with God through Jesus Christ) has an important role in your life, in that it is subject to come under attack and take a whipping, but it has the capacity to help you arise and keep on ticking!

Just as Jesus was grabbed, beaten, crucified, wrapped up and taken down into the earth, he arose as the chief cornerstone with all power in his hands so that you as a believer may have the same power to arise. Lay him as the chief cornerstone foundation in your life and recover from the disappointment, hurt, sorrow and embarrassment felt from falling down. Get back up, stand on the firm foundation which is Christ and bring into captivity every Potiphar's wife (tempting situation) that rises up against the purpose of God for your life! Recover, so you can encourage somebody else to do the same!

Spirituality & Sexuality

A Godly Perspective

7- Lay the Chief Cornerstone

As you enter the final chapter of this book, it is very important to understand that Jesus Christ is the standard by which you must choose to frame your life. No other foundation can be laid as the footing for a meaningful and purposeful life journey. Just as the cornerstone is the key component that holds a structure together, so is Christ the cornerstone (**IT**) foundation which holds the individual together. **Christ** the cornerstone equals (**IT**).

As a carpenter lays the foundation in the building process, you must lay Christ the cornerstone (**IT**) as the foundation in your own life. In other words, you've got to BRING the mindset and functioning of JESUS CHRIST strong and hard into every aspect of your life (i.e., spiritually, psychologically, financially, educationally, and occupationally) and *maximize* the *opportunity* God has for you to produce greatness! God's expectation for the brothers is to point

(**IT**), and sisters release (**IT**) in the right direction and don't let (**IT**) slip through your hands and waste to the ground!

For the brothers, a good example of this can be found in **Genesis 38**, which talks about Judah, the ancestor of Jesus. Judah was the tribe of Israel chosen by God to usher in the genealogy of Christ. In other words, this tribe had the responsibility of preserving the cornerstone (**IT**) foundation. The chapter opens with a brief description of Judah's family which consisted of his wife, three sons and a daughter in law. Upon the death of his oldest son Er, Judah in accordance with Jewish custom, instructed his son Onan (**v.8**) to marry Er's wife Tamar and raise up seed to preserve the family tree.

Onan was presented with an opportunity to produce greatness by furthering the lineage of Christ the cornerstone (**IT**) foundation. But because Onan knew that the seed should not be his, he became selfish, and whenever he went in to have sex with Tamar, he spilled (IT) on the ground (**v.9**). The natural (IT) in this story is the male reproductive fluid, but more importantly is the spiritual

(**IT**).... the **opportunity** to further the lineage of Christ. Onan failed to deliver by allowing the opportunity to slip through his hands and fall to the ground. This form of functioning in the secular is called masturbation. It's a behavior where you become the master of you own life, turn yourself in the wrong direction, take the bait of your flesh and spill God's given opportunity on the ground.

For Onan, it was a sexual challenge, but wasted opportunity can occur in many different areas of life. Brothers, whatever wasted opportunity you're sinking in, I encourage you to lay the cornerstone (**IT**) foundation in that area of your life, cry out to the Lord and believe that he has the power to lift you up! Don't let your past or others hinder you from accomplishing your Godly purpose. Complete the good work God has begun in you and don't let (**IT**) waste to the ground! I hear the Lord telling you to, **"BRING IT!"** You may be disappointed, hurt, embarrassed and filled with sorrow but, **"BRING IT!"** If Moses (slew an Egyptian), Abraham (lied on occasion), Jacob (was a schemer), Judah (slept with a prostitute), Joseph (hated by his brothers) and David (struggled with lust) could bring (**IT**) and each of them had challenges in life, then you can bring (**IT**) too! You were born to bring (**IT**)! You were created to bring (**IT**), and Christ died so that you could have the opportunity to bring (**IT**)! What or who are you waiting for? You can lay no other foundation than the one that has already been laid for you, and that is Jesus Christ himself! He has got to be the (**IT**) in your life! Go ahead right where you are and clap your hands and give God the praise for the chance to recover from wasted decisions and missed opportunities!

An example for the sisters can be found in **Luke 7:36-50**. This is the story about a woman who had an encounter with Christ while he was attending dinner at a Pharisee's house. It is said that the woman was a prostitute, which indicates that she tends to release herself in the wrong direction quite frequently, thus allowing her life and self-worth to spiral out of control and waste to the ground.

As Jesus was reclining at the dinner table, the woman

approached him. What is wonderful at this point in the story is the fact that the woman did not allow her lifestyle to keep her from approaching Christ. Sisters do not allow wasteful living to hinder you from drawing close to Christ. He came to minister to those who feel life has been slipping through their hands.

It's also important to note that the woman was familiar enough with Christ to recognize that he had what she was looking for; the capacity to restore her inner value which had been eaten away by the dynamics of her life. As she embraced the moment of, "This is who I am, in comparison to who you are Jesus, I humble myself before you" she began to weep. Just as a carpenter mixes the fluid of water with concrete powder to produce a firm foundation, so was she preparing the footing foundation of her restored life by **releasing** the fluid of her **tears** upon the feet of Jesus (**v. 38**).

No longer was she releasing herself upon barren ground, but now she was starting to bring (**IT**)! I truly believe that when a sister recognizes an opportunity for inner value to be restored, she will go above and beyond to lay the right foundation for the restoration process. The lady echoes my point by going beyond the traditions of the time and **released** her **hair** in public and began wiping the feet of Jesus and then she took it one step further and **released kisses** upon his feet and anointed them with fragrance as a form of worship. Now understand she was no stranger to letting down her hair and releasing herself, but a least this time she released herself to the right one!

Sisters stop releasing yourself to others who can't add value to your life. Take a page out of this woman's story and lay the cornerstone (**IT**) foundation!

The beauty of this story is the woman recognized that she was dirty, so she released herself on the dirtiest part of Jesus's body…his feet…. and then wiped them clean, thus signifying to him, *"I know you can wipe the dirt off of my life, just like I am wiping the dirt off of your feet with my hair, and I'm willing to take the fragrance that I would normally waste and put on for my clients and invest it all into you because I believe that you will invest your all into me! ..and the part of my life that is a stench to God right now, through my faith in you will become a sweet smelling fragrance to him once again!"*

This sister was bringing (**IT**) strong and hard! It doesn't matter what you've done in life or where you have been, what God is looking for is a sister who will release herself to him by any means necessary in order to obtain the legitimacy and self-worth that can only come from him. Because while others in the room were questioning why he was letting this continue, Jesus told her in (**vv. 48,50**), *"Your sins are forgiven. Your faith has saved you; go in peace."* My sisters release yourself to God, who has already released himself right back to you in the form of Jesus Christ, the cornerstone foundation! Lay (**IT**)!

Ultimately, laying the (**IT**) foundation involves answering the knock of Jesus Christ at the door of your heart.

Revelation 3:20 says, *"Behold, I stand at the door, and* *knock: if any man hear my voice, and open the door, I will come in to him and will sup with him, and he with me."*

What that verse simply means is that Christ desires to have a relationship with you. He wants to come into your heart and share with you his peace, love and joy. However, you must be willing to open your mind and heart to him.

Remember just as Christ stands at the door of your heart, so does temptation. It comes as a traveling salesperson carrying a mixed bag of stuff (**1Corinthians 6:9-10**). Don't answer the door to that craziness! But, let Christ come in and teach you what real, practical, victorious living is about.

As we conclude this journey, I pray something has been written in this book to broaden your perspective on the topic of relationships, spirituality and sexuality. While some of the subject matter discussed is sensitive in nature, if it is in the Bible, then we have an obligation to discuss it. Often the subject matter that is talked about the least, is the one people need to hear about the most from a Godly Perspective.

ABOUT THE AUTHOR

Pastor Kelvin K. Lucas- husband, father and Leadership Coach- grew up in Rocky Mount, NC. As a student attending Rocky Mount Senior High School, his journey towards servanthood began when he obtained his first job at the age of 16 at a local retail store. From that time, he began to embark upon learning a trade that has spanned for over 25 years and has taught him the essential key to empowerment...SERVING.

After attending North Carolina State University in Raleigh, North Carolina where he received a B.A. Degree in Business Management with a concentration in Marketing, Pastor Lucas took his trade to the next level by accepting a corporate executive position with a major retailer. Through those years he learned the leadership dimensions that would transition him into the next season of his life.

He was ordained as an Elder in July 1999, and in 2001 co-founded Take it By Force Ministries, a 501© (3) organization that offers community outreach events, leadership, creative writing and life skills training for youth and young adults (www.takeitbyforce.net).

Pastor Lucas truly understands the meaning of servanthood and has taken that passion to the community as a recreational sports coach, parent leader within the educational system and mentor within the community at large.

He and his wife, Felicia have been married since 1997, have three wonderful children, and are the Pastors of Dominion Tabernacle in Rocky Mount, NC.

Notes

Notes

Contact Information

Website: www.simplykelvin.com

Facebook: Simply Kelvin Lucas

Instagram: Simplykelvinlucas

Twitter: @Simplyklucas

Made in the USA
Middletown, DE
08 June 2023